every teenager's
little black book
on reaching your dreams

by blaine bartel

every teenager's
little black book
on reaching your dreams

by blaine bartel

Harrison House
Tulsa, Oklahoma

08 07 06 05 04   10 9 8 7 6 5 4 3 2 1

Every Teenager's Little Black Book on Reaching Your Dreams
ISBN 1-57794-627-8
Copyright © 2004 by Blaine Bartel
P.O. Box 691923
Tulsa, Oklahoma 74179

Published by Harrison House, Inc.
P.O. Box 35035
Tulsa, Oklahoma 74153

contents

contents (continued)

Planning

Sweat

contents (continued)

3 WAYS TO DISCOVER WHO YOU ARE

Perhaps one of the greatest journeys that you'll ever take is the one that leads you to the discovery of who God created you to be. You have a unique personality and skill set that God has given you. Many young people fail to realize all that God has made them to be. Here are 3 things to remember in this exciting journey.

1. **You will be incomplete without Christ.** Maybe you recall the memorable scene in the Tom Cruise movie "Jerry McGuire" when Tom finds his wife whom he had separated from earlier and says to her, "You complete me." Just as God puts two people together in marriage, you are to be married to Christ. Without that ongoing relationship with Jesus, you will always come up short.

2. **Study carefully what God has said about you.**

   The Bible is full of Scriptures that describe the attributes and character that He has for you as a person. The Word of God is like a mirror. (James 1:23.) When you look at it and commit to do it, you take on the character of God.

3. **Talk to family and friends about your unique personality.** Many times other people see things in us that we fail to recognize. You may be a great organizer, counselor, leader, giver, creator, or helper, and people around you will see that more quickly than you most of the time.

4 WAYS TO DISCOVER WHAT YOU CAN DO

Proverbs 18:16 promises, "A man's gift makes room for him, and brings him before great men." Believe it or not, God has put special gifts of ability in your life. Here are 4 ways you can find out what they are.

1. **Seek God in prayer, asking Him to reveal your abilities.** Jeremiah 33:3 tells us when we call upon Him, He'll show us things to come.

2. **Ask people close to you.** Solicit the evaluation of friends, parents, teachers, coaches, and others you trust to give their observations on your gifting.

3. **Go after things you have in your heart.** Never be afraid to step out and attempt something you've never done.

4. **Faithfully do the little things you are asked to do, the things you don't like as much.** God promises to give you bigger things when we do the small stuff well. (Matt. 25:23.)

7 ABSOLUTES OF GOD'S WILL FOR YOUR LIFE

Have you ever heard someone say, "God moves in mysterious ways"? I sure am glad that statement isn't true. The will of God doesn't have to be mysterious. Here are 7 things you can absolutely count on.

1. **God's will is salvation.** Our heavenly Father desires that all of humankind have eternal life with Him. That includes you.

2. **God's will is dominion.** Dominion simply means control. God wants you to apply His Word and take control of your body, thought life, attitude, and future.

3. **God's will is discipleship.** We are to grow in our walk with Christ. As we mature we are to help others do the same.

4. **God's will is unity.** Your words and actions must be united with God's Word.

5. **God's will is stewardship.** We are to take proper care of our time, money, abilities, and all God has entrusted us with.

6. **God's will is relationships.** Through the power of relationships, you will be able to accomplish things that would be impossible if you were alone.

7. **God's will is progressive.** God has a plan for your life that will be completed one step at a time, not in leaps or bounds.

4 THINGS TO LOOK FOR IN A MENTOR

A mentor is critical in the life of every successful person.
Joshua had Moses. Elisha had Elijah. The disciples had
Jesus. Oftentimes, mentors won't seek you out—you'll have
to find them. Here are 4 clues in finding the right one for you.

1. **A good track record.** Look for someone that has a
   good history of success in the thing you want to do.

2. **Mutual benefit.** Every great relationship will be
   good for both people. It is never one-sided. What can
   you do to help this potential mentor, bringing benefit
   to them?

3. **Unforced relationship.** Allow the mentoring relationship to develop naturally. Don't try to force

someone into this. Just find a way to be around them by serving, helping, and contributing any way you can.

4. **Ask the right questions at the right time.** Don't overwhelm this person to the point they want to avoid you. Be sensitive to the right opportunities to learn. Most of the time, you'll learn more by observing them.

7 SCRIPTURES TO GUIDE YOUR FUTURE

Can you imagine going into an uncharted forest without any map or compass? You might be lost for years. Many young people are living lost lives because they have thrown down the compass of the Word of God. Memorize these Scriptures. Pray them over your future and let them guide you.

1. **Jeremiah 29:11:** "For I know the thoughts that I think toward you, says the Lord, thoughts of peace and not of evil, to give you a future and a hope."

2. **Jeremiah 33:3:** "Call to Me, and I will answer you, and show you great and mighty things, which you do not know."

3. **Joshua 1:8:** "This Book of the Law shall not depart from your mouth, but you shall meditate in it day and

night, that you may observe to do according to all that is written in it. For then you will make your way prosperous, and then you will have good success."

4. **Proverbs 18:16:** "A man's gift makes room for him, and brings him before great men."

5. **Ephesians 3:20:** "Now to Him who is able to do exceedingly abundantly above all that we ask or think, according to the power that works in us."

6. **2 Timothy 1:9:** "Who has saved us and called us with a holy calling, not according to our works, but according to His own purpose and grace which was given to us in Christ Jesus before time began."

7. **Ephesians 5:15:** "See then that you walk circumspectly, not as fools but as wise."

[INSPIRATION]

3 THINGS TO DO WHEN YOU'RE FEELING LOW

Feelings come and go. We don't have the power to stop feelings of discouragement, worry, or depression from coming. But, we do have the power through Christ to overcome those feelings and move forward in life. Here's how.

1. **Memorize 3 good Scriptures that you can quote out loud to yourself.** Romans 10:17 says our faith comes on strong by hearing the Word of God! Three Scriptures I like to quote regularly are 1 John 4:4, Romans 8:31, and Ephesians 3:20.

2. **Put on some inspirational music.** We all have different music that inspires us and lifts our spirits, but I believe the very best is worship music because it is filled with the Word of God and helps your spirit commune directly with His.

3. **Get your mind and body active.** Someone once said, "Idle time is the devil's workshop." One of the tools in that workshop is the thought of discouragement. When you're active, your mind is focused on the task at hand.

3 THOUGHTS TO ELIMINATE FROM
YOUR THINKING

The Bible teaches us in 2 Corinthians 10:5 to cast down every high thought that would try to exalt itself against the knowledge of God. The act of casting down must be aggressive and then followed with replacement thoughts that encourage your walk with Christ. Guard carefully against these thoughts.

1. **"No one cares about you."** This temptation towards self-pity is a lie. People do care, and most importantly, God cares!

2. **"You won't succeed."** You have every reason to be confident if you are walking with God. Philippians 4:13 says you can do all things through Christ who strenghthens you.

3. **"Just give up."** Jesus didn't quit on you. He doesn't have a quitting spirit and He didn't put a quitting spirit in you. Persevere and finish the race!

4 WAYS GOD GIVES YOU DIRECTION

Do you need direction? Good, because God wants to give it to you. The direction of God is not hard to come by. Here are 4 ways He will give it to you.

1. **The Word (Bible):** the most practical way that God gives you direction. All other ways must line up with this way.

2. **Peace:** how God will lead you. His peace will be deep down inside letting you know you're headed in the right direction.

3. **People:** pastors, teachers, parents, and friends. God will speak through these people whom he has strategically placed in your life.

4. **Desires:** what you want to do. Do you like making art, building, or helping others? God has placed desires in your heart to help give you direction.

3 SECRETS TO BEING INSPIRED EVERY DAY

Inspiration in our lives can come from a variety of places. God has a wonderful way of using different things to get us moving in the right direction. Here are 3 secrets that inspire me in my day-to-day work and relationship with Him.

1. **The power of music.** Although my sons will tell you that my radio is usually tuned into sports-talk stations, I have learned to let music inspire me on a fairly regular basis. Whether it's a great new worship CD or just a song that stirs the soul, music has a unique way of lifting you up.

2. **The power of a book.** What you are doing right now is incredible. Congratulations! You are one of the few Americans that have taken time today to read a book. Of course, the Bible is different from all other books

and should be in our regular reading, but other books also have the power to launch us forward.

3. **The power of people.** The *right* people, that is. Like the pastor of my church each week when he preaches, or my colleagues in ministry who push me to new heights in my career, or my parents, my best friends, and my own family who help me take new ground every day.

3 KEYS TO MOTIVATING YOURSELF
TO DO DIFFICULT THINGS

The easy things come easy, don't they? It's easy to be motivated to play our favorite sport, shop at our favorite store, or eat our favorite dessert. But how do we motivate ourselves to do the hard things like the day-to-day work at school or home, regular exercise, eating right, or any activity that you know you should do, but everything inside of you says "No"? Here are 3 keys I've picked up along the way to motivate myself.

1. **Just start.** There is something magical about forcing yourself to "turn the ignition key" and get things going. It will give you that little bit of momentum to get rolling in the right direction. Make yourself start!

2. **Keep the end result in mind.** The Bible says in
    Proverbs 29:18 (KJV), "Where there is no vision, the
    people perish." If you don't remind yourself why you're
    working, exercising, praying, reading, etc., it will
    become too easy to quit. Motivate yourself with a
    vision of what this activity is going to accomplish.

3. **Reward yourself.** Create some kind of reward that
    you are going to give yourself for completing this task
    or activity. If might be watching your favorite show,
    getting a smoothie, taking a nap, or something else
    you like to do. God rewards us for doing right, so why
    not reward yourself!

[PLANNING]

3 PROBLEMS OF THOSE WHO DON'T PLAN

Planning is one of the great secrets of success in any area of life. The great thing is this: the God we serve already knows how the future is going to look so He can help us plan better than anyone else. Sadly, there are people who try to "wing it" in life. Here are 3 problems awaiting those who fail to plan.

1. **You are setting up a life system for failure.**

   You've probably heard the old saying, "Those who fail to plan, plan to fail." A lack of planning is actually a game plan to lose in life. Unprepared people are always unsuccessful people.

2. **You'll never inspire others to follow you.**

   People are afraid to walk in the dark. Ultimately, you are going to want people to help you get where you want to go. When people fail to see a plan for where you are going to take them, they are most likely not going to sign up for the ride.

3. **You'll give up more easily.** A plan gives you the approval you need to reach your goals and a definite finish line. A visual finish line will help you give 100% towards getting to where you want to go.

4 STEPS TO A PLAN THAT WORKS

The Bible tells us in Psalm 37:23 that the steps of the righteous are ordered of the Lord. A good plan isn't accomplished in just 1 or 2 huge leaps that get you there quickly. It is going to take time and it is going to take multiple steps. Here are 4 steps that are necessary for a successful plan.

1. **Write down your goals.** You cannot develop a plan when you haven't clearly established what you are trying to accomplish. It's got to be more than "I want a job." What kind of job do you want? What hours do you want to work? What kind of skills do you have? What work environment are you looking for? Be clear about your goals.

2. **Consult with people who have been where you want to go.** This may involve taking a person to lunch

or visiting them at their workplace. Perhaps you'll have to read a book or attend a seminar. Get the information you can on their journey to achieve success.

3. **Put together the resources to make your plan happen.** It may mean saving money, buying a weight set to train so you will make the football or soccer team, or simply writing down each resource and tool you'll need and figuring out how you are going to get them and use them.

4. **Be realistic on the time line.** We often try to bring our grandest plans to pass too quickly. Give your plan the time it needs and don't quit until you get there.

8 GOALS TO REACH BEFORE YOU'RE 18

At every stage in life, it is important to learn to set incremental goals towards the fulfillment of your dreams and vision. I encourage you to write down your goals as a regular reference point for your progress. Here are 8 goals to consider attaining before you're 18.

1. Make a long-term financial investment in the stock market.

2. Read the Bible through entirely.

3. Hold down one job for at least 6 months—a year if possible.

4. Read Dale Carnegie's book *How to Win Friends and Influence People.*

5. Obtain a basic idea of what career direction you are going to take, and make the necessary plans for school or training.

6. Develop one strong friendship that you will keep for life, no matter where you both end up.

7. Save enough money to buy a decent used car.

8. Keep your grades up, and get your high school diploma.

3 KEYS TO FORECASTING THE FUTURE

Your plan is always an experiment with the future. A good plan that has any hope of being fulfilled must have accurate forecasting of the future. What field of work will be most valuable to you and others in ten years? What is the next big idea in your area of expertise or interest? If you'll follow these 3 keys, the Lord will help guide you into a successful future others may find dim.

1. **Spend time daily in prayer.** Jeremiah 33:3 promises that if we call upon the Lord, He will answer us and *show us* things to come.

2. **Remember that history repeats itself.** A careful study of history will help us properly anticipate the future. In the early 1900s, people were calling for the U.S. Patent Office to be closed since everything had

already been invented and it was unlikely anything new or helpful would come along! This was before airplanes, computers, television, and a million other things. The lesson of this piece of history is to never close your mind to the possibility of change—in any area.

3. **Two heads are better than one.** I've found that I forecast better when I knock heads with my colleagues or coworkers. Challenge each other to dream and think outside the box called "today."

4 SCRIPTURES TO PRAY OVER YOUR PLAN

I believe it is very important to pray the right things over the plan that we make. The Word of God tells us in Proverbs 16:9, "A man's heart plans his way, but the Lord directs his steps." We need to take the time to devise a plan, but as we pray God will direct each and every step to get there. Oftentimes these steps aren't even in our original plan set forth. Here are 4 Scriptures I pray over all my plans.

1. **Mark 11:24:** "Therefore I say to you, whatever things you ask when you pray, believe that you receive them, and you will have them." Believe that you receive your desired goal by faith.

2. **Psalm 37:4:** "Delight yourself also in the Lord, and He shall give you the desires of your heart." Delight yourself in the Lord daily and your desires will be granted.

3. **Proverbs 21:5:** "The plans of the diligent lead surely to plenty, but those of everyone who is hasty, surely to poverty." With diligent work your plan will make you rich.

4. **Galatians 6:9:** "And let us not grow weary while doing good, for in due season we shall reap if we do not lose heart." Have a persevering spirit, knowing that you will reap if you don't give up.

[SWEAT]

4 WAYS TO GET HARD WORK DONE
MORE QUICKLY

Very few of us actually enjoy hard work. That's why it's called "hard work"—because it's hard. The harder the job, the more likely people are to put it off. The longer it is put off, the harder it usually becomes to complete. Just because it's hard doesn't mean that it is not worth doing or worth doing well. Here are 4 ways to get the hard work done more quickly.

1. **Break down the job into steps.** Making the big job several smaller jobs will help you see the progress along the way. Breaking it down will also help you decide how long it will take and what you will need to accomplish the task. Taking a small amount of time at the front will save you time in the long run.

2. **Start right away.** Procrastination only makes the work much more agonizing once you start. Don't let yourself think about how much you dislike the task, or what you would rather be doing. Just start somewhere; you can't finish something that you never begin.

3. **Find out if there is a better way.** Don't just search for a faster way to work; look for the best way. Doing things the right way will always save you time. Cutting corners may seem to help speed things up, but you don't have to re-do something that was done correctly the first time. It is always a good idea to look for the latest and smartest ways to do a job. Sometimes there may be a better tool or technique that could help you finish faster and end up doing a better job too.

4. **Recruit help when appropriate.** If a job is your responsibility, or if you are expected to complete the

work, do it yourself. If you can have help and the help is available, use it. Don't be so proud that you waste time on something that could have been done in half the time if you would have let others help.

3 REASONS "WORKING HARD" LEVELS THE PLAYING FIELD

There is no substitute for hard work. Working hard will open doors of opportunity that would not have been available otherwise. The greatest achievements do not always belong to those who have the highest score, but the people who are willing to work hard accomplish great dreams. Those who are busy working will quickly surpass those who have a head start financially or socially but refuse to combine hard work with lofty ambition. These are 3 reasons why "working hard" levels the playing field.

1. **Talent cannot work hard.** Talent will take you far, but many talented people have failed because they didn't work. Working hard can help make up for a lack of talent and put you in a position to succeed. Even if you are the most talented person in your field of

choice, if you sit still you will get passed by someone who is hustling to make things happen. Talent is like a seed; if it is not active, it cannot grow.

2. **You can't steer a parked car.** If you try to turn left in a car that is parked, you won't get very far. In order to make choices and navigate through life, you need to be moving. Working hard, no matter where you are, ensures that you are in motion and able to choose the right path. (Prov. 12:24.)

3. **Hard work makes up for your background.** No matter where you came from or what kind of family you have, if you are diligent you will be successful. People want to be surrounded by those who are passionate and will work hard to make each endeavor a success. Others will go out of their way to involve you, if you make the choice to be faithful and industrious. Your

willingness to work hard and finish a job will be far

more attractive than your family name. (Prov. 10:26.)

5 QUALITIES OF A VALUABLE EMPLOYEE

I currently have about 20 full-time employees and interns who serve under my direction and leadership. Each one of them is extremely important and valuable in contributing to our youth ministry. Here are the 5 qualities that make workers valuable.

1. **Diligent.** They give you 100 percent of their effort 100 percent of the time.

2. **Smart.** They think as they work, always coming up with better ways to get the job done more effectively.

3. **Faithful.** They take just as much pride in and give as much attention to the small details of their work as they do big things.

4. **Loyal.** They speak well of you, fellow employees, and the organization to others and always seek what is best for the organization.

5. **Productive.** They get results, are careful with the finances, and help the organization grow.

3 REWARDS ONLY FOR THE DILIGENT

How can you keep up your hard work along the way? One of the keys is to keep your eyes focused on the rewards you will receive for the diligent work of your hands. These rewards aren't just for anyone; they are unattainable to the lazy, slothful, and those who hope to coast to their goals. Be diligent.

1. **Promotion and opportunity.** The Bible says that if we are faithful to put our hand to work in the little things that we will be made rulers over much. You'll never get much unless you do the little. (Matt. 25:23.)

2. **Respect and recognition.** Who doesn't want other people to speak highly of you and what you've accomplished? Diligent people will always be highly favored and find a place of honor wherever they go.

3. **Wealth and windows.** Companies and organizations pay good money to people who work hard and work smart. Money always follows a diligent hand and so will windows. Windows are new ventures and ideas you've never seen before that hard work has opened your eyes to.

4 BIBLE VERSES TO HELP YOU WORK BETTER

God's Word has much to say about the way we go about our work. There is a right way and a wrong way to do everything, including the labor of our hands. Here are 4 critical thoughts to remember when we put our hands to a task.

1. **Our work is ultimately for Jesus Christ, not man.** The Word of God says in Ephesians 6:5 that even when our natural boss isn't looking, the Lord sees and inspects all that we do.

2. **Our work must be planned out well.** Proverbs 21:5 says the *plans* of the diligent make you rich, not just being diligent. So make sure you are working smart, using wisdom to get your job done in the most efficient way.

3. **Our work should produce results.** It's not just about producing a few beads of sweat. Make sure you are accomplishing something in what you do. Colossians 1:10 tells us to be fruitful in every good work.

4. **If we don't work, we won't eat.** (2 Thess. 3:10.) Work is an exchange of your valuable time for your bosses', customers', or clients' valuable money. The old saying, "There's no free lunch," is true. Life is an exchange every day. What you put out determines what will come back.

[NETWORKING]

3 SECRETS TO MAKING NEW FRIENDS

Everyone wants to be liked. That is no different in the "work world." People want friends and they want to be friendly, even those who seem a little "stuck up." Networking is really just the process of meeting new people and making new friends. People are your best resource as you work toward your career, so here are 3 secrets that will help you network and make new friends.

1. **Be friendly.** It seems obvious, but many people get so focused on the task in front of them that they miss the people and possible relationships passing them by. Grab each opportunity to build new relationships by doing the small things that make it happen. Say hello, introduce yourself, or simply smile. Make the first effort by showing yourself friendly. (Prov. 18:24.)

2. **Focus on others.** People want to talk about things that matter to them. If you spend 4 hours talking about your last doctor's appointment to someone you just met, don't be surprised if they start avoiding you. Make the effort to find out what they like and focus on things that you have in common.

3. **Do kind things without looking for credit.** The simple principle of sowing and reaping works in friendships too. If you begin to go out of your way to sow into the lives of people, you will begin to reap the kind of friends that you want. (Gal. 6:7.)

4 STEPS TO BUILDING STRONG RELATIONSHIPS WITH THE FRIENDS YOU ALREADY HAVE

Sometimes the hardest relationships to develop are the ones you have for a long time. It can be easy to take them for granted because it seems like those people will simply be there forever. Those people that you are closest to will be the biggest influence on your life, so developing these relationships is critical to your future. Here are 4 steps that you can take to make those relationships stronger.

1. **Be the kind of friend you want.** Sitting around wishing that your friends would treat you better is only going to wear out the couch. Start treating your friends the way you want them to treat you, and you will begin to see them treat you the same way. (Matt. 7:12.)

2. **Ask questions.** Be proactive. Find out how your friends are doing. Ask them about the things that they are involved in. Focus the questions on things you know they talk about, and be prepared to listen or help.

3. **Offer your help when needed.** No one likes to ask for help; offering your assistance will go a long way with your friends. A strong friendship means being ready to lend a hand to the projects and needs of others without making them beg or feel like they owe you a huge debt.

4. **Be an encouragement.** Try to be as supportive as possible of your friend's ideas or ambitions. You don't have to support dangerous or immoral ideas, but when it's within reason, offer your support. Don't be too quick to laugh or criticize, try always to be your friend's biggest cheerleader.

6 STEPS TO FINDING FAVOR
IN THE WORKPLACE

God wants to help you succeed in all your work. Your success in your job and career will be a direct result of your ability to get along with people. One of the coolest things in the world is having a job you love and working with people you really like. Here are 6 steps to get you there.

1. Don't treat your boss one way and everyone else a different way. People will see your hypocrisy and resent you.

2. Never cheat your company or business by stealing. I'm not just talking about their products or supplies; this also includes their time. If you're constantly late to work, taking long breaks, or leaving early, it's like

stealing money out of the cash register, because "Time is money."

3. Don't try to destroy someone at your work in order to get that person's position for yourself. It will eventually backfire, and you'll be out!

4. When someone else does a good job at your work, compliment the person personally and in front of your boss.

5. Never try to take authority or leadership that hasn't been given to you. Just do your job, and stay out of business that isn't yours.

6. Always give 100 percent. If you can give 110 percent, you were never giving 100 percent in the first place!

3 THINGS TO REMEMBER WHEN
YOU DELEGATE A TASK

Delegation is one of the best ways to multiply your effort. It allows you to be in many places, accomplishing many things at the same time. But delegation is not a "self-cleaning appliance." It does not take care of itself. A job that you delegate is not automatically completed. Here are 3 things that you should remember to successfully delegate any task.

1. **Be detailed.** Just because you know what needs to be done to complete the assignment doesn't mean that the person you are delegating the job to will know everything that you do. As you outline the work, be as specific and detailed with your expectations as possible. This will help you save time by avoiding lots of little questions along the way.

2. **Set a deadline.** If you give someone work to do, tell him or her when you want it done. Many people will wait until they absolutely have to start before they begin to work. If you set a deadline, they will know exactly when you expect it to be done, and you will not have to constantly ask them when they will be finished.

3. **Follow up.** If you are not the one doing the actual work, you should set a specific time when you can inspect the project. Checking the progress of a job will help you avoid problems along the way. If you make a habit of inspecting what you delegate, you will ensure that the work is done with the excellence you need.

4 WAYS TO MAKE A RELATIONSHIP "WIN-WIN"

Being involved in a relationship that is one-sided can be incredibly frustrating. You don't want to be constantly giving and giving without receiving anything from that relationship yourself. Every healthy relationship is mutually beneficial; it is good for both sides. These are 4 ways to make every relationship a "win-win."

1. **Start with you.** The best way to ensure that your relationships are not one-sided is to avoid the things that drain your friendships. Make sure that you are not being selfish or self-centered. Begin to look to do things for others before you expect things to be done for you.

2. **Know your limits.** Decide ahead of time what you are willing to do and what you will not. If you know

your limits and what your priorities are, you will avoid

getting into situations where you feel that your friends

have taken advantage of you.

3. **Be willing to say "no."** Just because you say "no"

    to certain things, doesn't mean that you are saying

    "no" to the whole relationship. The sooner you decide

    that you cannot do everything for everyone, the sooner

    you can relax and trust that kindly saying "no" will

    allow you to do the things that are important to you

    and avoid the things that waste your time.

4. **Be quick to say "yes."** Saying "no" to certain

    things will help you manage your time, but that doesn't

    mean that in a healthy relationship you never say

    "yes." In order to develop a good relationship you

    must be quick to say "yes" when you are able or when

    others have a need.

[OPPORTUNITY]

3 SMALL THINGS THAT CREATE
BIG OPPORTUNITIES

Small things make a big difference. Just like you probably
don't think about windshield wipers or toilet paper until you
need them or you run out, the small things in life often get
overlooked in the big picture of day-to-day living. Taking time
to pay attention to these 3 small things may help you avoid
pitfalls and create big opportunities.

1. **Go the extra mile.** People often miss great opportu-
    nities because they only do enough to get by. Make the
    choice to do the little extra things no matter how many
    people notice. Do everything with excellence. Try to be
    the best at what you do, even if you are doing some-
    thing that seems meaningless. Attention to detail and
    doing the little extras may be exactly what will open up
    a big opportunity for you.

2. **Keep your eyes open.** Observation is one of the best tools to success. As you are faithfully doing what you know to do, keep your head up and looking around. Don't get so busy and robotic that you walk right past your greatest success. It may simply be a better way to do what you are already doing, but if you have your head buried in the sand, you will miss many wonderful opportunities.

3. **Never quit.** The only thing you do when you quit is leave that much more victory for everyone else. The greatest achievements have come to those who have hung in the fight the longest. You can't create opportunities by sitting on the bench, so make the choice to keep going, no matter what happens or how many times you get knocked down.

4 KEYS TO MAKING THE MOST
OF A NEW OPPORTUNITY

New things are always exciting, but if you are not careful you can begin to place too much importance on your new opportunity. Remember, what you are doing is not the end of the road. Even though you might be really good at what you do, you have not arrived at the final destination. The best reward for doing something well is always the opportunity to do even more. These are 4 keys to making the most of a new opportunity that will help give you the opportunity to keep doing more.

1. **Ask questions.** As you step into a new opportunity, ask what is expected of your new responsibility. Find out what the goals are for the project or organization. Ask about deadlines, schedules, and things that you will be expected to take care of. Be as detailed as

possible; this will help you avoid the unknown and give you a head start toward making the new opportunity a success.

2. **Learn how the new opportunity operates.**

Whether it is a new company, project, or just an added responsibility, learn the policies and procedures before you begin. Learn what is accepted and what is considered rude. Find out how to communicate with your boss about what you are working on. Study the guidelines or mission statement, so you can make sure that you are not going in a different direction than what is important to them. Taking the time to find out the culture of the new opportunity will save you embarrassment and confusion while helping you have favor with your supervisors.

3. **Don't try to be the hero.** When you arrive in a new opportunity, it is often because you were considered to be good at what you do. In an environment with new people or just new responsibility, it can be easy to feel like you have to prove yourself to everyone involved. One of the best ways to make the most out of the new opportunity is to relax and be natural. You don't have to save the world overnight. Do your very best at everything you do, and the opportunity to voice ideas and make suggestions will come.

4. **Work hard.** The more opportunity you receive, the more grateful you should become and the harder you should work. Those who stop working when they advance are those who stop advancing. If you want to make the most out of a great opportunity, roll up your sleeves and start working.

5 DECISIONS YOUNG PEOPLE MAKE THAT SABOTAGE THEIR FUTURE

Who you are now and who you will be is determined by the decisions you make. One out of every one person will make decisions. When you have to make a decision and don't, that is in itself a decision. So the question is, what kind of decision-maker are you going to be? To help keep you from sabotaging your future, here are 5 decisions *not* to make.

1. **Disobey your parents.** God has placed your parents in your life to help guide you.

2. **Make quick decisions.** Before making a decision, take time to think it over.

3. **Develop wrong relationships.** The people you spend time with probably have the most influence on the decisions you make.

4. **Wait for your big break.** You must get off the couch and pursue your God-given destiny.

5. **Give up.** Both winners and losers face challenges, but winners don't quit.

4 OBSTACLES THAT COME WITH
EVERY GREAT OPPORTUNITY

Great opportunities do not come without challenges. Often, the greater the opportunity, the greater the challenge will become. If it were always easy, people would be walking into something new all the time, and you would never hear anyone complain about never getting a break. Preparing now to meet those challenges will keep you from being surprised and give you courage to overcome each one. Here are 4 of the biggest obstacles that come with every opportunity.

1. **Sacrifice.** If people only did the same things that have always been done, we would still be living in caves and using leaves for clothes. Great advancements come when someone is willing to sacrifice, because they are passionate about what was possible. Whether it is time, energy, money, fame, or popularity, as you set your

priorities you will have to sacrifice certain things to make the most out of any great opportunity.

2. **Knowledge.** Many times the full potential of an opportunity is never realized because the people involved simply didn't know enough. That fact has kept many people from trying to accomplish great things. As you undertake any great opportunity, there will be times when you feel like you just don't know enough, but that doesn't mean that you are not the right person for the job. Make the choice now to study and surround yourself with wise people and you will succeed where others have failed, even if you don't always immediately know the answer.

3. **Distraction.** There is so much going on in the world and so many things that try to grab your attention. If you don't choose to stay focused, you will get tripped

up by one of the biggest obstacles to opportunity. Those who can maintain their focus and see vision through to reality are the people who will be able to seize the opportunity and make the most of it.

4. **Fear.** The single biggest obstacle to success of any kind is fear. Fear will cause you to freeze and question if you really can do anything at all. Fear can make you say "what if" instead of "why not." If you allow yourself to look at opportunity through eyes of fear you will watch each opportunity pass you by and miss the great rewards of making a stand. God doesn't want you to react out of fear; He wants you to enjoy all the blessings of moving past that obstacle and making the most out of your opportunities. (2 Tim. 1:7.)

3 MENTAL MISTAKES THAT DENY
YOU OPPORTUNITY

Whether it is a school you want to be admitted to, a job you would love to have, or just a promotion, there are mistakes that you can make that will cost you the opportunity you desire. Many mistakes are obvious, but others are mistakes that people make every day and do not even realize that they are losing opportunities by not thinking through the choices they make. These mistakes are mental mistakes. Here are 3 major mental mistakes that can deny you great opportunity.

1. **Leaving projects un-finished.** Big projects take weeks and even months to complete, but daily tasks should be finished right away. When people constantly have to finish what you start, they will eventually stop trusting you with anything important. No one likes doing your job for you, and "I forgot" will only

work once or twice. Make yourself daily checklists and think through the little things that may not seem big to you but show the people around you big things about your character.

2. **Making choices without permission.** Often, opportunity will be given based on trust. You can miss that opportunity if you make choices without going through the proper chain of command. It can be easy to forget to ask, and sometimes it may seem like extra work, but it is a little extra that can go a long way toward proving that you are trustworthy.

3. **Complaining.** Watch what you say. People complain and then wonder why they don't get the promotion they wanted. If your supervisor notices that you complain about everything, they will think twice about how you will talk about them when they are not around.

Sometimes it is natural to talk about the things that went wrong or a decision you didn't like, but show loyalty with your words if you want people to trust you.

PRAYER OF SALVATION

God loves you—no matter who you are, no matter what your past. God loves you so much that He gave His one and only begotten Son for you. The Bible tells us that "...whoever believes in him shall not perish but have eternal life" (John 3:16 NIV). Jesus laid down His life and rose again so that we could spend eternity with Him in heaven and experience His absolute best on earth. If you would like to receive Jesus into your life, say the following prayer out loud and mean it from your heart.

Heavenly Father, I come to You admitting that I am a sinner. Right now, I choose to turn away from sin, and I ask You to cleanse me of all unrighteousness. I believe that Your Son, Jesus, died on the cross to take away my sins. I also believe that He rose again from the dead so that I might be forgiven of my sins and made righteous through faith in Him. I call upon the name of Jesus Christ to be the Savior and Lord of my life. Jesus, I choose to follow You and ask that You fill me with the power of the Holy Spirit. I declare that right now I am a child of God. I am free from sin and full of the righteousness of God. I am saved in Jesus' name. Amen.

If you prayed this prayer to receive Jesus Christ as your Savior for the first time, please contact us on the Web at **www.harrisonhouse.com** to receive a free book.

Or you may write to us at:

Harrison House

P.O. Box 35035

Tulsa, Oklahoma 74153

MEET BLAINE BARTEL

Blaine Bartel is one of America's premiere leadership specialists. Blaine served as Oneighty®'s Youth Pastor for 7 years, helping it become America's largest local church youth ministry, reaching more than 2,500 students each week. He is now the National Director of Oneighty® and Associate Pastor of 12,000-member Church On The Move in Tulsa, Oklahoma. Blaine has served under his Pastor and mentor, Willie George, for more than 20 years. God has uniquely gifted him to teach local church staff and workers to thrive while faithfully serving the vision of their leader. Known for his creativity and respected for his achievement, Blaine uses the *Thrive* audio resource to equip thousands of church and youth leaders each month with principles, ideas, and strategies that work.

Past: Came to Christ at age 16 on the heels of the Jesus movement. While in pursuit of a professional freestyle skiing career, answered God's call to reach young people. Developed and hosted groundbreaking television series, *Fire by Nite*. Planted and pastored a growing church in Colorado Springs.

Passion: Summed up in three simple words, "Serving America's Future." Blaine's life quest is "to relevantly introduce the person of Jesus Christ to each new generation of young people, leaving footprints for future leaders to follow."

Personal: Still madly in love with his wife and partner of 22 years, Cathy. Raising 3 boys who love God: Jeremy—19, Dillon—17, Brock—15. Avid hockey player and fan, with a rather impressive Gretzky memorabilia collection.

To contact Blaine Bartel,

write:

Blaine Bartel

Serving America's Future

P.O. Box 691923

Tulsa, OK 74169

E-mail: bbartel@churchonthemove.com

Or visit him on his Web site at:

www.blainebartel.com

To contact Oneighty®, write:

Oneighty®
P.O. Box 770
Tulsa, OK 74101
www.Oneighty.com

OTHER BOOKS BY BLAINE BARTEL

Ten Rules to Youth Ministry and Why Oneighty®
Breaks Them All

Oneighty® Devotional

every teenager's
little black book
for athletes

every teenager's
little black book
on how to get along with your parents

every teenager's
little black book
of God's guarantees

every teenager's
little black book
on how to win a friend to christ

every teenager's
little black book
on sex and dating

every teenager's
little black book
on cash

every teenager's
little black book
on cool

every teenager's
little black book
of hard to find information

little black book
for graduates

Additional copies of this book

are available from your local bookstore.

Harrison House

Tulsa, Oklahoma

www.harrisonhouse.com

Fast. Easy. Convenient!

- ◆ New Book Information
- ◆ Look Inside the Book
- ◆ Press Releases
- ◆ Bestsellers

- ◆ Free E-News
- ◆ Author Biographies
- ◆ Upcoming Books
- ◆ Share Your Testimony

For the latest in book news and author information, please visit us on the Web at www.harrisonhouse.com. Get up-to-date pictures and details on all our powerful and life-changing products. Sign up for our e-mail newsletter, *Friends of the House,* and receive free monthly information on our authors and products including testimonials, author announcements, and more!

Harrison House—
Books That Bring Hope, Books That Bring Change

THE HARRISON HOUSE VISION

Proclaiming the truth and the power

Of the Gospel of Jesus Christ

With excellence;

Challenging Christians to

Live victoriously,

Grow spiritually,

Know God intimately.